When I began reading *When God Came Calling,* I could not lay it aside. If you have ever wondered how you can find God or even speculated about another person's journey toward God, you will enjoy reading Treva's book. She has skillfully written a personal, inspiring story that kept me walking alongside her from the first page to the last.

—Susan Dalton Bullion
Human Service Assistant

Treva Denas writes from her heart to touch the hearts of her readers. Her compelling life story is so well written you will not want to put this book down. Even with all of the tragic events in Treva's life, she was able to keep sight of Jesus. God never turned his back on her, allowing a happy ending to her amazing story. May you receive God's richest blessings from reading Treva's story, *When God Came Calling.*

—Patricia Ann Hall
Risk performance specialist

I found Treva's book, *When God Came Calling*, to be exceptionally written, very inspirational, and motivating. When Satan tried to complicate her life, Jesus kept stepping in to simplify it. This book will be a joy to all that read it, and they will know that God wants everyone to receive his free gift of salvation.

—Donna Elliott
Trauma intake

WHEN GOD CAME CALLING

a story of undeserving mercy and grace

WHEN GOD CAME CALLING

a story of undeserving mercy and grace

TREVA DENAS

Tate Publishing & Enterprises

When God Came Calling
Copyright © 2009 by Treva Denas. All rights reserved.

No part of this publication may be reproduced, stored in a retrieval system or transmitted in any way by any means, electronic, mechanical, photocopy, recording or otherwise without the prior permission of the author except as provided by USA copyright law.

Scripture taken from the New King James Version®. Copyright © 1982 by Thomas Nelson, Inc. Used by permission. All rights reserved.

The opinions expressed by the author are not necessarily those of Tate Publishing, LLC.

Published by Tate Publishing & Enterprises, LLC
127 E. Trade Center Terrace | Mustang, Oklahoma 73064 USA
1.888.361.9473 | www.tatepublishing.com

Tate Publishing is committed to excellence in the publishing industry. The company reflects the philosophy established by the founders, based on Psalm 68:11, *"The Lord gave the word and great was the company of those who published it."*

Book design copyright © 2009 by Tate Publishing, LLC. All rights reserved.
Cover design by Lance Waldrop
Interior design by Stefanie Rooney

Published in the United States of America

ISBN: 978-1-61566-266-1
1. Biography & Autobiography, Personal Memoirs
2. Religion, Christian Life, Spiritual Growth
09.09.15

Dedication

To my heavenly Father, who is a God of second chances and gave me the inspiration and courage to write this book.

> O God, you are my God; early will I seek you; my soul thirsts for you;
>
> my flesh longs for you in a dry and thirsty land where there is no water.
>
> So I have looked for you in the sanctuary, to see your power and your glory.
>
> Because your loving kindness is better than life, my lips shall praise you.
>
> Thus I will bless you while I live; I will lift up my hands in your name.
>
> Psalm 63:1–4 NKJV

Acknowledgments

I want to humbly thank my pastor and his wife for being willing to review my book as I attempted to write my story of *When God Came Calling*. They were very excited for me and felt that I had an awesome testimony to share with the world.

I want to thank my family and friends for encouraging me and lifting me up in their prayers that this book would be read by the people that need hope and encouragement. My family, friends, and their friends are waiting for their autographed copy of *When God Came Calling!*

This book is also in memory of a wonderful woman of God, Carolyn Spence. I had the privilege to be with her as a companion during her final six months of battling cancer. During our time together, we would talk about our "days gone by," and as she learned more and more about my days gone by, she told me that I needed to write a book. It so happened that I had been working on a book and had it with me, and I gave it to Ms. Carolyn to read. She was the first person to know about my attempts of writing a book, and once she read the rough copy, she said, "You have got to finish this book and get it printed for others to read about the grace of God and to know there is always hope." She would always encourage me to "get it going" because my book, *When God Came Calling,* needed to be out and available to people. There will always be a special place in my heart for Ms. Carolyn and the advice and encouragement she gave me.

Foreword

As a pastor, I deal with traumatic episodes on a regular basis. When I heard that Treva had been in a terrible automobile accident, I pictured in my mind what it could have been like—but nothing could have prepared me for the photographs that I saw. As I looked at the pictures, all I could think was, *there is no way that she should be alive right now. God must have protected her.*

Those who are struggling ask, "Why is God allowing me to go through this?" In this compelling book, Treva Denas helps to answer this question, acknowledging God's presence in the midst of terrible trials. Her powerful testimony of God's divine intervention during her near-fatal accident will leave you with feelings of inspiration and hope.

—Pastor Craig Polston
Kingdom Baptist Church
Fredericksburg, Virginia

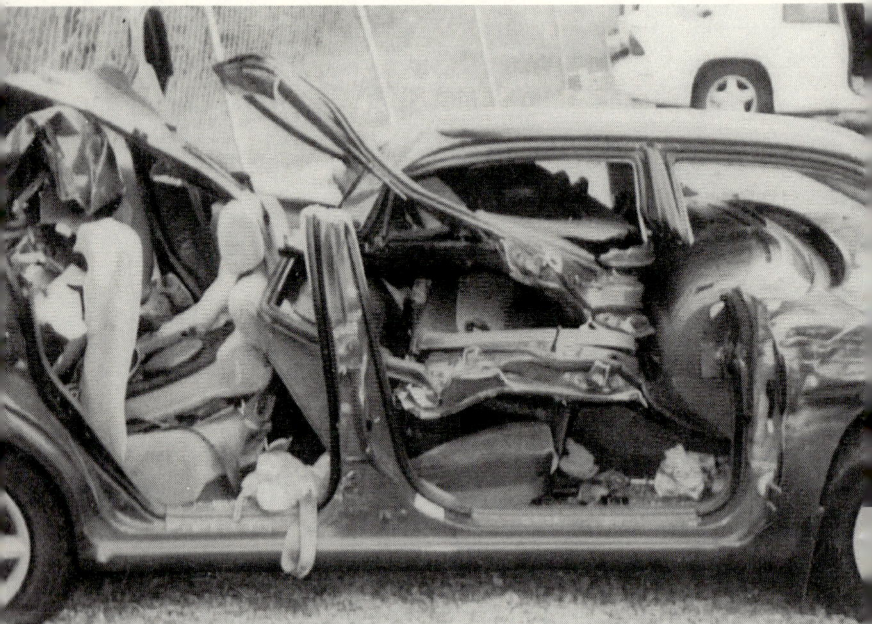

Introduction

When God Came Calling is a book about renewing our hope, our trust, our faith, and our relationship with God. How often do we feel we have lost all hope in God? How often do we feel that our relationship with God is just a mockery? How often do we find that the trust and faith we once had in our Savior is no longer there and stays just outside our reach?

We feel totally unworthy, useless to a point; our hearts feel numb with a lack of emotions, and we just go through the motions of everyday life. Even though we think our emotions are on hold, we are surprised that we can feel some pain when we think there is nothing God can do for us to help us out of this hopelessness, and even if there was, why bother?

Then something happens, and you cry out one more time for God to help restore your hope, your trust, your faith, and your relationship with him, thinking that maybe, just maybe this time will be different than the last. You begin to realize your trust in God had never really disappeared but went on a detour, and you had to be reminded to look for it in the farthest, darkest, and deepest crevice of your heart, body, and soul.

My encouragement to you is to realize that once God saves your soul, you are his child forever and ever, amen!

> My sheep hear my voice, and I know them, and they follow me. And I give them eternal life, and they shall never perish; neither shall anyone snatch them out of my hand. My father, who has given them to me, is greater than all; and no one is able to snatch *them* out of my Father's hand.
>
> John 10:27–30

Satan has little ways of intervening and getting us off track, and at times we seem to go so willingly. Usually before we know what has happened, our relationship with God has tumbled quickly, and doing God's will is just a dream—again. Satan laughs at us because he knows that we are weak and if we keep falling, each pick-me-up will get harder and harder as we feel worse and worse about failing God. Often we take our failures and totally give up all thoughts about being a servant of God, until he intervenes with an attention getter.

I did not have to recover from severe injuries, as most of my healing had to come from within my heart and soul. I could have ignored this accident as being *"in the wrong place at the wrong time"* situation. However, I chose to believe this was a direct intervention from God.

This book is very simple for anyone to read, from high schoolers to senior citizens, and I pray that each one of you that is struggling will see yourself somewhere in this book and know that God can and does change us. Maybe you have already read every hope, love, and mercy book you could get your hands on, and it hasn't helped any. Every encouragement book is different, and I pray there is something in my book that you can relate to that can and will help you. This book is written from my past, my trials, my heart, and with God's guidance.

I actually started this book while recovering from my auto accident when God laid it on my heart to write a book about my life. I felt he was leading me to share with others how I came to realize that God is the God of hope and second chances, not just for me but for everyone. I was at the point of my life when all I wanted was a lukewarm relationship with God. It was like I wanted to keep him in the closet on standby and do things my way first, and if that did not work, then I would ask God to help. Of course, God does not work that way, as our life is not our plan but God's plan. As you read this book you may realize that you are just a stone's throw away from your own wake-up call. Perhaps by sharing my trials, my hurts, my joys, and my experiences with you, I can help you avoid a life-threatening wake-up call.

I really thought writing this book would be fairly simple, not realizing I would have to dig deep in past emotions, which I had attempted to forget about. I have also been hesitating finishing this book because I am no eloquent writer. It terrifies me that perhaps God's future plan is to have me speak to various groups about this book. I am no speaker, but then God reminded me what he told Moses, so I can only trust God if it comes to that privilege.

Then Moses said to the Lord, "O my Lord, I am not eloquent, neither before nor since you have spoken to your servant, but I am slow of speech and slow of tongue." So the Lord said to him, "Who has made man's mouth? Or who makes the mute, the deaf, the seeing, or the blind? Have not I, the Lord? Now therefore, go, and I will be with your mouth and teach you what you shall say."

Exodus 4:10–12

Before I start with the story of my accident and the aftermath, I would like to ask you readers to walk with me down memory lane. The reason is that I feel for everyone to be able to really understand and comprehend how this accident changed my relationship with God, I need to start from my childhood and move forward to the present. I would also like to share with you how I got to the stage of my life where God, in his infinite wisdom, felt that I needed a wake-up call like I have never had before to open my eyes and heart.

Because I am now a senior citizen, I have a lot to tell you before you will get to my story of the accident and the day *When God Came Calling*. I am hoping you will sit back, get a cup of coffee, maybe a tissue or two, and walk with me as I tell you about the long journey it took me to really hear God and to realize there is hope. Hope he gave me to accept that I am truly, truly loved by the most awesome God. A God who is a forgiving God regardless of what I, and you, have ever done. Walk with me as I fail again and again to get right with God, yet he never gave up on me. Walk with me and see how God allowed a semi to smash into my small vehicle the day *When God Came Calling*.

Chapter 1

He's going to hit me! As I looked in my rearview mirror while stopped in traffic and saw this big truck traveling faster than it should have been, I knew this was not going to be good. On that revelation of a note, I was in for the ride of my life. This ride would take me on a journey where I would have to deal with severe pain, tears, why-me questions, a few pity parties, and most of all, my lukewarm relationship with God. When all was said and done, I would end up being given and shown so many awesome blessings from God during my time of healing. It is amazing what God will allow to happen to open our eyes to what is really important, and that is our daily walk and relationship with God.

In my fifty-two years, I have weathered many trials, a lot that I brought on myself through my stubbornness and what *I* thought *I* wanted. However, nothing had prepared me for what was to happen on that beautiful day, April 11, 2006. Looking back, I am thinking I should have called in sick at work and stayed home for the rest of my life! But I am sure that God would have had a plan B to deliver my wake-up call.

I was born in 1953 in southwest Virginia being number seven of seven with three brothers and three sisters. For some reason, Mom named most of us kids with odd names, and I wanted to share them with you in order of oldest to youngest. They are: Elwood, Marbrie (Birdie), Wavie (Wade), Troy Laymon (Butch), Hillis (Hill), Bettie (Bet), and Treva (tee-toes). We were raised in a three-room house on a minifarm where we were taught to work hard in order to survive. We had cows that my parents had to hand milk twice a day regardless of the weather. We kept what we needed, and the rest of the milk was sold to provide an extra income to buy necessities. We also made our own butter from the cream that we would scoop off the top of the milk after it settled. The calves would be sold to also provide money for whatever necessities were needed, which usually was for shoes and clothing before school started each year. We had hogs that were slaughtered every fall for food.

We had chickens to provide eggs and a Sunday dinner from time to time. We always had a big garden or two to grow our own foods.

We were kept warm by wood stoves that were in the kitchen, living room, and back room. The boys slept out in the building we called the shanty, and it also had a wood stove in it for warmth. It was usually us kids that had to restock the woodpile on the porches regardless of the weather. To this day, I still love the smell of wood burning in stoves and/or fireplaces.

My mother was a stay-at-home mother, and although she was busy from dawn to dusk, she was never too busy to help a neighbor out. She was more than willing to help them with the seasonal canning, working in the garden, or even washing walls sooted from the winter fires.

My dad worked in the saw-milling business, which depended upon the weather. He also helped with the chores when he was able to get home before dark. Sometimes the timber he was cutting was away from home, and he would be away during the week and home on the weekends. This left my mom and us kids to do the necessary chores around the house, plus help with the milking. We did not have a lot of things, but we had what we needed. I remember a song that said, "We didn't know we were poor because the grass around our house was always green."

As horrible as it may sound to some of you, Mom would sew a lot of our clothes out of the cloth feed bags. These cloth feed bags were made from pretty fabric, which once washed, dried, and ironed no longer looked like feed bags. She would use the white ones to make sheets or pillowcases. My mom never threw anything away and usually was able to reuse whatever it was for other things.

Winter meant that it was time to start quilting quilts. Mom would start cutting out quilt pieces from fabric she was able to get throughout the year then sew them together until she had the top. Then a call would go out to the neighbors and family that it was time to put in a quilt to be hand quilted. This was a time where the women were able to be together and catch up on all of the local news and/or country gossip. These women worked hard on their own farms, and to be able to get away to join neighbors for quilting for a few hours meant relaxation, lots of talking, and good food.

I remember Mom would let Bet and I play

under the quilt while they quilted, as long as we did not get in the way, and we would pretend it was a cave or a house. When they were done for the day and all the ladies had returned back home to do their own chores, we would pretend it was a bed for our baby dolls. We would also bat the spools of thread from side to side just to see how far they would roll—ah, such simple entertainment! When the first quilt was done, Mom usually had another one to go in, and that is how the winter went for us while we waited for spring to start the outside work all over again.

Of course, being the baby of the family allowed me to get away with a little more and not having to work as hard as my older brothers and sisters had to. As each one became legal age and graduated and/or quit school, they normally left home. As the children dwindled, so did the need for my parents to have humongous vegetable gardens and lots of farm animals, and over time they became less and less until it finally ceased completely. Of course, the work that needed to be done on a daily basis was hard, and it kept us busy most of the time, but we had fun too.

In the wintertime, we used to have a lot of

snow, and we kids would walk to the top of the hill in the field across the road and ride cardboard boxes down the hill in the snow. We would walk to the store in the snow—there was never too much snow to go to the store and get a candy bar or peanuts or a soda pop. We also would tie a rope around an old tire and pull it on the snow to make a little path to the outhouse or to one of the other out buildings. There usually was a kitty cat or two that would hop on for a ride. We were kept busy carrying firewood to the porch to keep the fires going for warmth and for cooking.

In the summertime, some of the neighborhood kids from miles around often would get together on Sunday afternoons to play softball in an empty field. Usually it was me, Bet, Hill, Butch, and a bunch of our cousins. It did not matter if you were six years old or sixteen; everyone got to hit the ball. The afternoon would pass quickly, and it would be time to get home for chores and supper before we knew it.

From time to time, Bet and I would visit our cousins about a half mile away (yes, we did walk), and we would find things to do. I remember one of those things ended up being a corncob fight where

I got hit in the eye, and needless to say, that was the last corncob fight we were allowed to have.

We would also play store under the front porch by gathering up all of the empty containers we could find. For play money, we made our own by tracing and cutting out the coins—we never had dollars to buy anything with. Looking back, I sometimes yearned for the simplicity of it all.

Sometimes when we had a quarter or two, we would walk to the other country store about a mile away to buy a soda pop and a candy bar, and then we would walk back. Of course, back then we did not think anything about having to walk wherever we wanted to go—that was just the way it was. As we got a little older, I also remember some of those walks to the store were just a cover-up so we would have the freedom to experiment with things such as cigarettes, snuff, and chewing tobacco (sorry, Mom!). Let me tell you, we did not have to experiment too many times before we realized it wasn't for us.

I remember having a little red wagon. My sister and I would pull it up the hill; then we would take turns riding it down the hill and hope we would be able to stop it and not end up in the ditch. I also remember an old bicycle Bet tried to ride and ran into the shanty because she did not know how to put the brake on—that was so funny!

Summertime would mean the harvesting of the garden, the canning of the bounty in a hot kitchen with no air except what would blow in through the open doors. My mom canned everything she could get her hands on, and the cellar stayed full to be able to feed all of us. Everyone had to help when it came time to dig up the bushels and bushels of potatoes, something we had a lot of. They were kept in the cool cellar so they would not rot as we ate them throughout the year.

Oh, living out in the country and being poor, we were privileged to have an outhouse and no indoor plumbing. That was just the way it had always been, and we did not think anything about it. We got our water from the spring coming down the mountain, probably about 150 yards from the house. On washday, there were several trips to the spring. Eventually they ran the water from the spring down into the yard so it would be a lot closer, and it stayed that way for many, many years.

In the summer, we would put our glass bottles of pop in the cold water to keep cold, and on a hot summer day, there is nothing more refreshing than an icy-cold bottle of pop. We would also do the same thing for a cantaloupe or a watermelon, which we would buy from the traveling produce man. Running water and indoor plumbing was not something we had in the house until all of us kids were adults.

I remember that there was only one Bible in the house, and Mom kept it hidden in the linen closet to keep it from getting damaged. I never saw either of my parents read the Bible. Mom would get the Bible down to write in the births, deaths, and marriages, and she would put things in there that she did not want to get misplaced. As I got older, maybe ten to twelve, I do remember being curious and trying to read the Bible, but I just did not understand what I was reading. No one had ever shared with me the plan of salvation, and I did not even know what the *plan of salvation* was, but I was seeking.

"For since the creation of the world, his invisible attributes are clearly seen, being understood by the things that are made, even his eternal power and Godhead so that they are without excuse" (Romans 1:20).

Basically, the *knowing* that there is a God that created the heavens and earth is instilled in us when we are born; perhaps that is why I was searching. When I was growing up, the country churches were not opened every Sunday because the preacher was a traveling preacher. I never heard my parents or really anybody talk about God or about church, but it was a given that we would go to church when the preacher came into town. No one complained about going; it was just something we automatically did.

There were a couple of churches that we would go to, but the kids would stay outside and play while the adults would go inside. At that time there was no need to be concerned about the safety of the children, as the older ones looked after the younger ones. It was a tradition to go to one of the churches in the area on the third Sunday in August when there was dinner on the ground. I remember my mom, her mom, and her sister making enough food to feed all three families and then some. We would have fried chicken, green beans, mashed potatoes, cornbread, apple pies, banana pudding, and especially fresh, homemade lemonade. It doesn't get much better than being surrounding by family and neighbors and sharing your food on a beautiful Lord's Day.

My parents, especially my mom, instilled in me a sense of kindness, compassion, and helping others. It did not matter if they asked you for help; you just knew, and my mom loved to help other people every chance she got. She tried her best to teach us to be honest and to do what's right. As you get older, or I should say more mature, you realize that you were not as smart as you thought you were and that your parents pretty well knew what they were doing.

Life changed as I got older and reached that preteen era, which no one explained to me. My brothers and sisters got married one by one, moved away from home, and had children of their own until my youngest brother and I were the last ones to be living at home. You would have thought since I had most of my parents' attention I would have been in seventh heaven.

However, when I was almost thirteen, I got it in my head that I wanted to die, and I ended up taking a handful of aspirins. Why? I really do not know, because things at home were still the same. The only thing I can think of is that I had just gone through the trauma of appendicitis and I was in recovery mode. That surgery, plus entering into puberty, could have altered my attitude, I supposed. I just don't know, and of course I wished I had never done it. I vaguely remember that my dad met up with my sister Birdie that evening, and I stayed with her that night.

I told Birdie what I had done, and she got me the help I needed. I spent several months in a treatment center in Richmond for troubled children, where I was in therapy. When I was released, I went back home and returned to school, but I just could not get with it. I eventually went to live with my sister for a few years and continued my counseling.

While living with my sister and her family, we would go to a nearby church. I never felt that I fit in at this church, as I was very shy and uncomfortable around the other girls my age. No one told me why I went to church, and no one told me that I needed salvation. I just thought it was somewhere to go to get us kids out of the house for a few hours. I remember one Sunday the pastor was saying that Jesus would forgive us for our sins. I remember sitting in the pew and crying and wondering if Jesus would forgive me, but I still did not understand. I do know now that it was the Lord that was nudging me and speaking to my heart. I sometimes still wonder why someone did not tell me more. Why didn't the pastor see my tears and talk to me? I could have died that night, and I would have gone to hell!

I eventually graduated from high school and finally had my diploma in my hands! Out of the seven of us kids, I was only the second one—the first one was Birdie—that actually graduated from high school. My family was so proud of me, and I still remember the little graduation party they gave me.

Once I graduated from high school, adulthood came with a bang, and of course I was in a hurry to get on my own. To my way of thinking, I did not need anyone, and I wanted to be my own person. However, it did not take me long to learn that I did need my family to survive. I needed my dad to give me advice on my first vehicle. I needed my mom to give me food out of the garden and canned food from the cellar so I would have something to eat. I needed my sisters to give me advice and just be able to spend time with them. I needed my brothers to help me when my car broke down. I've learned that it does not matter how old you are, you still need your family!

I got an apartment and a job with a telephone company as a long-distance operator. Believe it or not, that used to be done manually. While there, I made several new friends, and one of them eventually introduced me to my husband to be. WT lived about forty-five minutes from me, and he was a country boy, which suited me just fine since I considered myself a country girl. I really liked his mom, dad, and his two sisters, and they liked me.

We dated off and on for a while, and WT eventually got a job closer to where I lived and moved in with me. At first it bothered me a little bit, but as my family got to know WT, I stopped feeling guilty about living together. However, after living together for a couple of years, we did get married and continued to live in a one-bedroom-apartment complex.

By then, I was working for an insurance company that handled various claims for people. As they expanded, they hired an extra clerical worker whom we always called KL. KL was sweet, polite, and likeable with a great personality. I soon found out she was a devout Christian that prayed before she would eat, talked about God, and spoke about her husband who taught Sunday school, but she never pushed her religion on anyone.

We both found out we were pregnant around the same time, and we each had planned to tell our employer that very day. I ended up telling them first, and then KL told them a few days later. She stopped working before her son was born to be a stay-at-home mom, and I lost contact with her. I found out later that our children were born within a week of each other.

My husband and I moved into a two-bedroom apartment a few weeks before our daughter, Melissa, was born on Christmas Eve. This apartment was at the top of a hill, and at the bottom of this little hill was a church. Prior to moving to the two-bedroom apartment, that particular church never interested me because I could not see it. You know what they say: "out of sight, out of mind." Now every time I looked out the window, walked out in the yard, or drove out of the complex, I couldn't help but see this church at the bottom of the hill. It got so that every Sunday for several months I would sit beside my window and watch people coming and going, and I would feel the overwhelming desire to go and be a part of that church. I did not because I disliked going places where I did not know anyone, and I just knew that I would feel out of place. I know now it was Satan telling me all those lies, as he would do anything to discourage me and prevent me from ever learning about the gift of salvation that God had to offer me.

After about nine months, I started thinking about contacting KL and inviting them over so we could meet each other's baby and spouse. I finally picked up the telephone to call her, and we planned an evening that would work for both of us. In visiting, it was mentioned that they went to church and invited us to go with them, but would you believe that they went to the church at the foot of the hill from where we lived! I'm sure my jaw dropped all the way to the floor! The exact same church that I would stare at every Sunday wishing I had the courage to go. Mmmm, what a coincidence. Or was it? Looking back, I can picture God with a big smile on his face when I moved to the apartment on the hill, when KL came to work for the same office as me, and when

I reconnected with KL. God already knew what was going to happen; it was part of his plan!

But still yet, we did not commit to go to church with them at that time. KL did call to invite us to come to church with them. I kept backing away, so she asked if she could take my daughter, who was about one year old, to church with her. I thought, *Sure, why not?* That went on for a few Sundays, and I finally told KL I would go with her the next Sunday, but she *had* to stay with me!

Of course I had nothing to be afraid of, as the people were wonderful and friendly, and I was made to feel welcomed. A couple of Sundays later, the pastor asked if I would like to meet with him and KL in his study and talk about salvation. Finally! I, a twenty-two-year-old woman, was going to actually hear about salvation for the first time in my life.

"For God so loved the world that he gave his only begotten son, that whoever believes in him should not perish but have everlasting life" (John 3:16).

The pastor explained God's gift of salvation and offered it to me, and I accepted. I found out later that KL had called the church's prayer chain so they would be praying that I would accept Jesus Christ as my personal Savior! To this day, I still remember the peace and joy that came over me, but it was the *peace* that was so overwhelming; there just did not seem to be words to express it.

"Therefore having been justified by faith, we have peace with God through our Lord Jesus Christ" (Romans 5:1).

"Now may the God of hope fill you with all joy and peace in believing that you may abound in hope by the power of the Holy Spirit" (Romans 15:13).

I was a new creature, I had *hope,* I had *joy,* I had *peace,* and I had the Holy Spirit living within my heart! Wow! When I returned home and told my husband about it, I still could not find the words to express the deep peace that was within my heart. I could hardly sleep that week because I was so excited about being God's child and so impatient to make my public confession in church the following Sunday. I was so afraid that God would come back before I had the opportunity to say, "Yes! I am a child of God!"

I quickly soaked up the Word of God like a sponge. A few months later my husband also accepted Christ, and we became a family going to church together. We were both baptized and joined the church. Our lives were filled with Christian friends, church, and God's Word in such a way we lived and breathed Christian influences.

My husband played on the church softball team every season. We had a few Bible studies at our apartment for people within the church to come to. I eventually taught the Wednesday night Good News Club for preschoolers, spent time being a nursery chairman, and held the position of the Sunday school superintendent for a while. As far as I was concerned, we were very happy and living off God's promises. Please don't get me wrong; we had our share of differences and arguments, but they seemed to eventually work themselves out and life went on.

About five years later our son, Dwayne, was born, also in December, and we moved to a three-bedroom apartment in the same area. Instead of being on the hill looking down at the church, we were just down the street about a half of a block. Now we were a standard family of four, working hard to make a living, provide for our children, and still were very much involved with our church.

Melissa accepted Jesus as her personal Savior when she was about eight years old. She kept pestering the pastor that she wanted to be baptized even though she was only eight years old, and *yes,* she *knew* Jesus lived in her heart. So after her birthday when she turned nine years old, the pastor agreed to baptize her.

When Dwayne was about the age of seven and we were driving down the road, he asked me how he could get Jesus in his heart. I had the privilege of telling him how, and he said he wanted Jesus to live in his heart that day! He went forward the following Sunday and was baptized a few weeks later.

Chapter 2

When the kids were about thirteen and eight, my marriage began to falter. Looking back now, I have to admit that both of us just quit trying, and when you quit trying, that pretty much means a death sentence. I also realized WT was seeing someone from his work and had been for a while. However, he could not make his mind up if he wanted me and the kids or if he wanted her. In the meantime, I still had my church behind me for support, and they were praying for us.

This was happening around the Thanksgiving and Christmas season, and I finally told WT that he had until the first of the year to make his mind up: was he staying or was he leaving? On New Year's Day, WT moved out, and that was that; his choice was made. The hardest part was telling our children that their daddy did not live with us anymore. I had to make sure they knew Daddy still loved them and they did not do anything to make him go away. Daddy had somewhere else to go and live, but he would see them whenever he could. How my heart broke to see my babies cry, as they just did not understand. Sometimes I still wonder if our marriage could have been saved if we both had not given up—maybe, maybe not. We still had not told his family, but his mom eventually figured it out. His mom has always been so precious to me, and I hated for her to find out like she did. But I just could not bring myself to tell her, and I guess WT couldn't either.

After WT moved out, I felt relieved because I could stop walking on eggshells. I could stop being so tense when he got home from work and having to watch my words to avoid an argument. I no longer had to lie in bed and listen to him talk to *her* on the phone in the living room. I considered myself a failure because I could not keep my marriage together. I had always dreamed that whenever I got married I would be the best wife and mother there could ever be, and we would be the perfect little family who would live happily ever after. When WT left, life would become a roller coaster of highs and lows, walking with

God, walking with Satan, and not knowing which one I would choose for that day.

"Watch and pray least you enter into temptation. The Spirit indeed is willing, but the flesh is weak" (Matthew 26:41).

At first I tried to watch, pray, and stay faithful to God to get through this period of life, knowing deep down inside my heart that he would take care of me and my children. I still remember receiving $5 in the mail that came *just in time* to buy some milk. My church had a food drive for me, which helped me keep food in the house. Another person set a budget up for me that helped for a while until I stopped using it.

Not long after WT left, Dwayne started having horrible behavioral problems at home but only in my presence. I kept searching for a way that I could help him, but nothing seemed to work. We eventually went to counseling, which helped for a while, but eventually nothing helped with his behavior. He was also not doing very well in school with his studies, and I kept pushing for him to be tested because I could feel there was something that wasn't quite right. He was finally tested and diagnosed with ADD, but he was not hyperactive. I was so relieved because finally the teachers would know that he needed extra help and patience. The doctor put him on Ritalin, and we saw a wonderful change in school with his grades improving drastically. However, his behavior around me was still very much an issue.

Melissa would shut herself up in her room and would give the evil eye to *anyone* that would dare to walk in her room except her best friend, Beth. Unfortunately, my daughter was unable to have a childhood per se because she had to grow up quickly after her dad left. She became a second mother to her brother by watching him after school at home so I could work late or watching him Saturday mornings so I could go in and work half a day.

But as time went by and I encountered so many problems, I just gave up. I was lonely, I was so overwhelmed and miserable, I was unhappy, and I was very, very tired. My children had emotional problems and I had emotional problems, so I basically turned my back on God and ran right into the arms of Satan. How could this have happened? It was simply because I had stopped depending upon God to see me through this part of my life and putting him first in my life. I stopped reading God's Word, I stopped praying to God, I stopped relying on God to supply my needs, and I stopped worshiping God.

"For my thoughts are not your thoughts, nor are your ways my way says the Lord" (Isaiah 55:8).

I began going out trying to find that *right person* instead of trying to do what was right for my children and me. I mean, I needed someone too, didn't I? No, not really, I needed to care for my children, and they should have been my number one priority. I was feeling that I was totally worthless, and why would God love a worthless person like me? Relationship after relationship came and went, and the only thing that changed was my son, who became angrier and physically aggressive. Tantrums were an everyday thing, and in trying to work though those, I ended up neglecting my precious daughter. Oh how she must have hated me and her brother. She was also going through her adolescent moments; there were quite a few rough spots for her, and I felt so inadequate and helpless.

I have to admit that there were days when I actually hated my son because of his behavior. But I know now it was more of hating myself because

I did not know how to help him. I hated myself because of the situation we were in and because we did not have money to pay bills and do things like other families.

I'm sure you, the readers, are shaking your heads as to how I could have done that. Did I not know better? What about everything I had learned about God? Where was my peace? Where was my joy? Where was my hope? Didn't I *know* that God would help me? I mean, all I had to do was to get down on my knees, ask forgiveness, and cry out to God for help—didn't I know that he would lead me though the valley if I let him? Where was my love and fire for God now? Nobody was happy except for Satan and his crew.

"Be sober, be vigilant; because your adversary the devil walks about like a roaring lion, seeking whom he may devour" (1 Peter 5:8).

This Bible verse is so true, and I hope you will believe me when I say that Satan does make house calls! When you give Satan an inch, he ends up taking a mile so he does not leave anything to chance. He is very crafty, deceptive, and sly, and he will find ways to make us believe his lies that keeps us in bondage to him and out of a relationship with God. Every time we take our eyes off God and his guidance, we fall, and every time we fall, it is harder and harder to get back up because Satan plays with our minds. We get defeated and discouraged because *we* see no way out and forget that God has a plan. We lose our joy because *we* start looking for *things or someone* to make us happy and ignore the joy that only God can give us. We get impatient and antsy until we finally throw up our hands and try to fix the situation ourselves, and *we* usually end up making it worse instead of waiting on God and his timing.

Satan rejoiced every time I gave up, and for every time I gave up, that made me one step closer to Satan and one step farther from God. I felt I had let God down so many times, and each time I promised it was the last time, and guess what? Here I am again, Lord! Why? Because I took my eyes off of my heavenly Father and focused on myself, my circumstances, and that is when Satan jumps at the chance he has been waiting for. He finally sees a crack in the armor, just a sliver, but enough to get in and start causing mayhem. Each time I let God down, Satan made me feel so dirty and depressed and think, *Oh, what's the use?* I kept thinking there was no way that I could go back to God and ask forgiveness *again* because this was the hundredth time, but I should have remembered that God is all about forgiveness.

"If we confess our sins, he is faithful and just to forgive us our sins and to cleanse us from all unrighteousness" (1 John 1:9).

I kept feeling Satan encouraging me to just forget it and stop the yo-yo feelings that I was having. Just live each day the way I wanted to and that way I would not have those yo-yo feelings. When you do your own thing, Satan doesn't need to keep after you day after day, minute after minute because he only has to give you the idea and then you are on his track. He just sort of keeps a watchful eye, and if we start thinking about God, he'll gently, or not so gently, nudge us away from that way of thinking. He does this by bringing our self-image down to a worthless and undeserving way of thinking and putting things in our paths so we do not have time, or the strength, to take the Bible and read God's Word.

I continued my journey without God, obtained my divorce, and life went on. I eventually met HS, and we were together for about two years. HS was a disc jockey on one of our local country music stations. He was a very down-to-earth person, but his life revolved around his second career of collecting vintage records—yes, I said *records*—and selling them to collectors throughout the world. However, he was not a family man and did not know how to relate to children; plus he had almost no sense of humor. If you have children, you have got to have humor! HS was unable to understand the emotional behavior of my son, although I will have to say that he did try to a point. He did try to be a big brother to my son. But HS did not know how and when to say no, and my son was able to really stress him out in a very short amount of time.

It's sort of ironic that my son thought a lot of HS. I remember one time we had gone our ways for a couple of weeks, and my son was looking out the window and happened to see HS drive up. He yelled, "HS is here!" and went flying down the steps, out the front door, and into his arms. That really made an impression on HS, but no magic wand was waved, and he did not automatically turn him into a father figure. It was about time to have the common sense to know that we would never make it as a couple. We both had different expectations of each other and different dreams. Eventually we both realized that it would not work out, and we gradually stopped seeing each other. Ah, another relationship down the drain!

During this passage of time, some of my church family continued to try to help us by encouragement, love, and support. However, as my choice was to continue to travel down the road of sin, the *help* was in the form of telling me what I should and shouldn't do, and I quickly grew very aggravated and tired of listening to their opinions. As I still lived down the street from the church location and almost directly across from the pastor's home, I could feel eyes on me quite often.

So I made the decision to quit going to church, not even thinking about my children's spiritual needs. Not even thinking that they, as well as I, needed to hear God's Word more than ever to give us hope and encouragement. How my heart breaks now when I think of how I let Satan control my thoughts, my mind, and basically destroy us as a family. It was as if all of the years I spent accepting God's Word, studying God's Word, and growing in God's Word evaporated directly in front of me.

The children and I still spent a lot of time with WT's parents and would often spend the weekends with them. I just had to call and make sure WT wasn't there or planning to be there with his girlfriend since I still was not too happy with him.

We also spent a lot of time with my sister Birdie and her husband, Jack, since they lived close by. We would go there quite often on the weekends just to get away from the house and allow me to focus on something else, rather than my situation. They, likewise, would drop by from time to time just to see if we needed anything or to drop off food from their garden.

To add to my emotional load during this time, our mother was in the hospital for tests, and Birdie and I found out that she had cancer. We barely had time to react before they wheeled her out to where we were waiting to go back to her room. We just sort of held each other up until we could get some time to ourselves to adjust to the news. From that point on, whatever weekends the children spent with their dad, I was spending with my parents to help my mom with things around the house and doing things that my dad was unable to do.

Mom's health eventually deteriorated to the

point where she became bedridden, and she was moved in with my sister to be closer to her doctors and the hospital. My sister worked next door to her home, so if she needed to run back over to the house, she could; plus her husband was on disability and was home most of the time, so my mom was never alone. We children, Mom's grandchildren, and Mom's sister would take turns being with her twenty-four hours a day, seven days a week to help her eat, drink, take her medication, and make sure she was all right.

It was very heartbreaking to see my mom in this situation, weak and unable to take care of herself. She had always been the backbone of the home, able to work rings around any of us and solve a lot of our problems, and now she was so weak she could hardly lift her head. At times, she did not even know who we were and did not understand why we called her mom. I'm pretty sure we girls shed a lot of tears behind closed doors because we were losing the mom we knew and loved. The only consolation we had was knowing that Mom was not in a lot of pain due to her cancer. I also knew she was ready to meet her Maker.

Mom was hospitalized in December of 1987

for the last time and eventually went into a coma. A family member was with her around the clock, and I was working at a company right across from the hospital, so I would pop in every day at lunchtime. On December 21, I dropped by to see my mom, and the nurse told us that her vitals were dropping and the family needed to be called. My sister, Wavie, was quite shaken, but I was able to stay calm enough to notify the rest of the family and tell them to get to the hospital.

Even though I had turned my back on God, I knew he was there with us and was keeping me calm and from falling apart until later when it would finally hit me. I also know God was in that room because the moment my mom took her last breath and joined the angels in heaven, the watch she was wearing also stopped at 4:05 p.m. and has never run again. My mom's long, hard journey was over on earth, and a new life was just beginning in heaven.

As time passed, my self-esteem hit rock bottom, and depression was an everyday thing. I was finally dealing with the recent death of my mom, the grief was so gut wrenching, and I felt I had nowhere to turn. I felt God would not want to hear from me again, and I had burned my bridges with God one too many times. I felt I had nothing to offer that would do God any good, and as far as I was concerned I was a nothing! Does this sound familiar?

However, according to the Word of God, he is in the business of forgiving sins. If God forgave me yesterday, he will forgive me today and tomorrow because he never changes. I knew that, but I was not at the point where I was ready to ask God to forgive me. I still wanted to do what I wanted to do, and I was not ready to give that control back over to God.

"Jesus Christ is the same yesterday and today and forever" (Hebrews 13:8).

> If we say that we have no sin, we deceive ourselves, and the truth is not in us. If we confess our sins, he is faithful and just to forgive us our sins and to cleanse us from all unrighteousness. If we say that we have not sinned, we make him a liar, and his word is not in us.
> 1 John 1:8–10

Chapter 3

Around Thanksgiving in 1988, a coworker introduced me to her brother, Charles (Chuck), who was separated from his wife and had one son, Chuckie. He lived about four hours away in northern Virginia and was coming to visit his sister for Thanksgiving. After I got off from work one evening, I went to her home to meet him. We practically talked all night, the time just flew by, and from that night on, we had a long-distance romance. What was I thinking? I guess the answer would be that I wasn't thinking. We would talk on the phone for hours almost every night after the kids went to bed. Some weekends he would drive down and spend the weekend. He got along well with my children, which was a plus. He was fun to be with and was very caring and supportive as he dealt with my children, especially my son.

I felt relieved that he apparently cared enough about me to try to help with my children and to encourage me throughout the week. It did not matter to me at that time he was only seeking adult companionship, was still married to his wife, and in a way still loved her. Of course he could not see that she was using him, and I just knew I could eventually change all of that.

He did bring his son, Chuckie, with him a couple of times, and I could tell he was a very materialistic child who revolved around name brands. The higher the price, the happier he was. I could also tell that my daughter did not care for him at all, and my son was just glad to have a boy to pal around with for a while. Nevertheless, their worlds were miles apart, as their interests were totally different at that time. Chuckie just could not understand why I did not live in a fancy home and why I did not have this and why I did not have that.

If I had really taken the time to look at the big picture, I would have seen that this relationship was not the best thing for my children and me, but I was past thinking what was best for the children and only thinking what was best for me. On the other hand, I had "someone" of the opposite sex who supposedly cared about me and gave up his time to drive four hours just to see me. I mean, that counted for something, didn't it? I thought he had to feel something more than us just being friends to continue these trips and telephone calls for several months. Right?

A couple of the ladies from the church did come by to "discuss" my living situation, as if it was any of their business. At that time I considered God's people to be a bunch of holier-than-thou people who had the nerve to tell me that the way I was living my life was wrong in the eyes of God. My mind, with the help of Satan, did not want to hear that. I rationalized my excuses not to listen to them. I mean, they had a spouse who loved them, they had two paychecks to make ends meet, they had children that were not out of control, and they had someone to fix their car when it broke down. How dare they try and tell me what I should and should not do because they loved and cared for me! I just wanted to be left alone by the church. They could find someone else to show the love of God to; I did not want it.

My only irate thought was, *How dare they?*

As our relationship continued to exist, my son's behavior continued to deteriorate, and I refused to acknowledge that perhaps this relationship was making it worse and be willing to give it up. It had gotten to the point where I just could not handle him. I felt so helpless in trying to deal with my son, and it seemed that nothing I tried worked for any length of time. I finally made the decision that his dad had to take him, as he did not throw tantrums around him, only around me. His dad felt I just wanted to be free to do what I wanted to do, which was not true at that time but would come later. I don't think anyone, except my daughter, realized how bad my son's tantrums were. It just was not a good situation between my son and me and getting worse every day. I felt I had done all I knew to do to try to help him, and it's not as if I did not get professional help—I did. I was at the emotional point that I realized if he did not go to live with his dad, something terrible would happen to one of us.

How could I give up my son, you ask? He was my own flesh and blood I carried and protected under my breasts for nine months. He was the ten-pounder baby the nurses called their little quarterback. He was my little sunshine baby that never cried unless he was hungry or sick. Did I not see he still needed his mother as though he was still an infant? Could there have been another option besides giving my son away to his dad? I have to admit there was something else I could have done—I could have sacrificed my wants and replaced them with my son's needs. I could have turned back to God for help. Somehow we could have made it, but instead I was so focused on my wants and needs I felt I had no other choice.

No one ever knew how it broke my heart into a million pieces to see him leaving with his bags packed. No one saw the tears I cried night after night because he wasn't there for me to tuck into bed at night and to hug and kiss him goodnight. No one knew I was unable to go into his room for a few weeks after he left. I just shut his door and tried to pretend he was spending some time with his dad or granny and would be back soon.

I continued my long-distance relationship with Chuck, and as our feelings started to change toward each other, we discussed the possibility of me moving to northern Virginia and living with him. At this point, I was ready for a change, but at what cost? This part of the book is where it gets really emotional and hard to write. This is where I have to relive emotions of almost twenty years ago to the time I abandoned my children so I could have a new life at their expense.

At the time I really think that Satan had numbed me to any feelings in giving my kids away. I do not think I was totally aware of what I was doing to my children or to myself. I know I was being very self-centered, thinking it wouldn't really matter that I wasn't with my kids and they would probably be better off without me. Satan had helped destroy my marriage, helped me to destroy my relationship with God, and now he was helping me to turn my back on my children. What a sly, cunning person he is. He made sure that I kept my eyes on *me* and what *I* wanted, regardless of the cost. As my son was already living with his dad, my daughter chose to live with her granny so she would not have to put up with her brother. She did not want to live with me because she did not care for Chuck's son, who she felt was spoiled rotten and a snob.

I am very ashamed to admit that I just assumed that Granny would not mind becoming her guardian and letting her live with her. It never crossed my mind that perhaps Granny would not be able to raise her granddaughter or perhaps she would not want to be tied down with a teenager. She had already raised her children, and then I come along and dump my daughter on her. Oh, how stupid I was!

I rationalized that since my children were with family that it would be okay to leave them. They did not need a mother that could not get her life together and they would be better off without me. When I made the decision to move to northern Virginia, I bet Satan had a party in my honor on the day I actually moved. I'm sure that God shed some tears on the day I left my children behind and made that final commitment to give up my children that he had given me to care for. I so hoped that God held and comforted my children as they were being left motherless. So, in April 1989, I was off for a new, exciting, happy, enjoyable, peaceful, and relaxed lifestyle—I thought.

I did talk to my children and family a lot on the telephone, and I would convince myself that everything was okay, until I hung up the phone. Then I would think, *What have I done to my children?* We did go down to visit with them quite often and bring them back with us for a weekend or holiday, but they were never that comfortable being in a strange house. Eventually, we all adjusted to the way it was, but underneath my adjustment was a big void in my heart that would not go away as the years went by. I kept telling myself what a fool I was to leave my children, what a fool I was to leave my family, and what a fool I was to leave my job. But Satan kept reminding me it was too late to turn back now, and I was stuck with my choice and was stuck without my kids.

I mean, what was I supposed to do, go back home without a job, no way to support my children, and yank them out of the new routine they had just adjusted to until my next relationship? I don't think so. Oh, the agony and heartbreak of wrong and selfish decisions when we try to run our own lives. On the outside we look as though we have it all together and we are happy and totally placid with life, but on the inside there is nothing but turmoil. This turmoil churns and churns and eats away at you until you give up because you feel as though there is nothing anyone can do and you have lost all hope. I should have remembered that God was not *anyone,* and he was waiting for me to realize I needed him, his forgiveness, and his help.

When I first met Chuck, it did not occur to me to talk to him about his relationship, if any, with God—heck, that was the farthest thought from my mind, and at the time, it really did not matter if he did or didn't have one. I did not even ask if he believed in God, thinking that if he didn't, I would be able to persuade him later on—yeah right! Here I was fighting against a relationship with God and at the same time thinking I could help Chuck eventually find a relationship with God. I guess I can say that I was totally confused and messed up.

I found a job with a plumbing, heating, and air-conditioning company. I was told that the owners were a Christian family, and that is the main reason I took the job, go figure. I was running from God, but I still wanted to be around people who called themselves Christians. This job was a big adjustment as I knew nothing about plumbing, heating, and air-conditioning, but I learned and actually enjoyed my job—on most days.

The owners were very caring for their staff and bent over backwards to help those that needed help. I saw their hearts of gold as they went that extra mile for a lot of people, me included, and I will always be very thankful and appreciative.

There were several times when I actually thought I could not live this way any longer and wanted to return home. I was so homesick, and I knew that God was not pleased with my living situation; plus everything was new to me, and I felt so alone. Several times, I would leave and just drive down some country road as I cried, trying to figure out what I was going to do, but always turning around and coming back. Chuck tried his best to support me mentally and emotionally and help me over the problems and roadblocks we had, but he just did not understand this *God thing* and why I would be so bothered about the way I was living. This was the eighties, almost nineties, and I needed to get a grip.

Since moving in together, we talked a little about religion, and I found his parents had raised their children in the Catholic religion. Our living situation did not bother him, and that was just the way it was. He was raised in a completely different type of environment with different rules and regulations. As he matured into a teenager, he basically did his own thing and tried to stay out of trouble, eventually marrying his first wife. They had a son, and he was baptized in the Catholic church they attended for a few years until they stopped going.

I'm surprised that my living situation did start to bother me, but I know the Lord works in mysterious ways. Even though I had purposely turned my back on the Lord, the Lord did not turn his back on me. There were times I felt so strongly the need to pack up my things and move back with my family, but by then I had fallen in love with Chuck and just could not do it. I was weak, so very weak, and of course, Satan was still stopping by every now and then to keep check on the situation. He surely did not want to see me get really serious about this *God thing*, and you can see that it worked.

There were Sundays I felt if I did not go to church I would go off the deep end. It was as if my soul was thirsting for God's words to speak to me, but yet, I never changed my sinful lifestyle. I wanted both sides of the coin; I wanted to worship God, pray to God, go to church, sing hymns, and expect my prayers to be answered, but not change my lifestyle. I wanted it all but on my terms, and God does not work on our terms.

During the year of 1993, my father became very ill and was in and out of the hospital quite often, and being so far from him made it very hard for me. Late one evening in November, I got word he was not doing well and suggested that I come to the hospital very soon. We arrived in the early morning hours on November 3, and he died several hours later after I got there. Once again, grief had hit our family that could only be healed as time passed by.

It had been five years since I had moved in with Chuck, and he was still married to his first wife and appeared to be in no hurry to get his divorce. It upset me greatly whenever she would call to talk to Chuck and get some advice on what she should do about something. I was of the mind that since she walked out on him, she could figure out her own advice or ask her boyfriend that she left Chuck for. I also realized that as they had a son together, she would be involved in our lives until their son graduated from high school, and that was something I just had to tolerate since I was the *other woman*. His son and I got along all right, as I tried to encourage him to study hard and behave himself, but he basically did what he wanted to do.

I could tell his wife was using Chuck, and it took a while, but his eyes finally opened and he realized the same thing. Divorce proceedings were started, papers signed and finalized. Chuck was once again a single person, and I was no longer living with a married man. But the situation still was not right, and here we went about this *God thing* again.

Was I happy? Was I content? Did I want to return home? Did I want to stay? Did Chuck love me enough to marry me? Did I love Chuck enough to marry him? Would Chuck ever ask me to marry him? Would Chuck ever start going to church regularly? Would Chuck ever publically accept Jesus Christ as his personal Savior? Would Chuck be willing to allow God to be Lord of his life? These were questions that ran through my mind day in and day out, and the only answer I could come up with was "I don't know."

I was still visiting churches to find one that felt warm and welcoming, and Chuck would go with me from time to time so I would not be by myself. Even though I was a backslider and did not have a good relationship with God, I still yearned to be around God's people and hear his hymns of praise being sung. I believe even then that God was working in my heart little by little.

Eventually we moved out of his townhome into a house we had built when I found out that I was able to buy a home as a first-time homebuyer. I was finally able to leave "their house" and live in "our house."

After moving, I starting looking for a church and located a Baptist church within five miles of home. Chuck went with me the first time we visited, and when I walked in, I had a sense of coming home and knew I had found my church. Of course, no one knew we were living together and not married, and that was something I was not going to voluntarily admit.

I started going regularly to church, and Chuck usually went with me. He seemed to enjoy the pastor's preaching, the services, and making new friends. As time passed, I kept praying that God would touch his heart and he would publically accept God's free gift of salvation, or if he had already been saved, he would make a public confession and be baptized, but he never did. At times I felt like he was fighting so hard not to make that commitment; why I do not know. It was very disappointing to me, but at least he was hearing God's Word being taught. I could only keep praying and hoping Chuck would allow his heart to be touched by the love of God where we could serve him together. Yes, you are reading correctly, all of this from the one who didn't need God or want God in her life when she really needed him the most.

Now that we all had time to adjust to all the changes that were made when I moved, life settled down into a routine. I was learning to feel better about myself and to *allow* God in certain rooms of my heart, but not all.

We lived together for ten years before he asked me to marry him. He proposed early on the morning after a Halloween night, and of course he had it all planned out. I was just getting up, and he said I needed to see what was outside. My heart sank as I figured that the kids had egged the house or done some other mischief during the night. I looked out the back door, and Chuck had spray painted in the grass, "Will you marry me?" in bright fluorescent orange paint! I was totally stunned, as I had sort of given up on the idea that we would ever get married. But I was able to get the "yes" word out, and we planned for an April wedding!

Since I needed to ask the church pastor to marry us, I had to confess to him that we had been living together. He was not pleased, of course, but we were going to make it right and he would be glad to marry us. Chuck and I married in April 1998 with both of our families in attendance and our children participating. Finally our relationship was made legal, and I was no longer *living in sin,* so to speak. Free at last! I thought, but no, not really because the Bible plainly states that believers should not marry unbelievers. Once again, I was doing what I wanted to do, not what I should do. I was thinking with my emotions, not with my heart.

> Do not be unequally yoked together with unbelievers. For what fellowship has righteousness with lawlessness? And what communion has light with darkness?
> 2 Corinthians 6:14

Ten years is a long time not to have a one-on-one relationship with God, isn't it? Ten years is a long time to be frozen in sin, isn't it? Ten years is a long time spent being disobedient, isn't it? Ten years is a long time trying to fill the void you have in your heart, isn't it? Ten years is a long time to attempt to hide your sins from certain people, isn't it? Ten years is a long time not to receive God's special blessings that had your name on them until you chose to no longer serve him, isn't it? Yes, I still struggle with the feelings of those ten years, and I wonder from time to time how God would have blessed my life had the ten years not happened. I wonder what the will of God would have been. However, the ten years were my free-will choice, and as the saying goes, "You made your bed; now you have to lay in it."

A few months after we got married, my church began to have problems, and a lot of people started to leave. We held on a few months, and then we left also. In the next year, we visited several different churches, and I knew that God would let me know when I had found the church he wanted me in. A deacon visiting us from one of the previous churches we had visited told me, "You may never find that church." I was really shocked to hear him say that, considering he was a deacon, because I knew that one day I would find a church like that.

During the years we have been together, Chuck could always tell when I needed to go home and see my family even though I tried to hide it. Whenever I would become withdrawn, quiet, teary eyed, and talk to my family every day on the telephone, he would casually suggest a trip to see my family. Each visit allowed Chuck to get to know my family better and my family to get to know him better. My family is full of humor, teasing and playing jokes on each other, and he was their victim quite a few times, which meant they liked him.

Chuck has always been there for me during the rough time of family illness and deaths, and I love him dearly! I did not realize how much his love and support would come to mean to me until I heard the "C" word after a yearly mammogram.

In April 2001, I was diagnosed with breast cancer. The sad part was that I had no home church to pray for me. Cancer ran in my family like water, and I knew I would have cancer one day. It wasn't a question of if; rather it was a question of when. I had gone for my annual mammogram, and the radiologist came back in for a couple of retakes. Before I left, she said that sometimes they have you come in for a CT scan, so I could be getting a telephone call. I knew then that they had found a lump, and so I waited. I really did not feel any fear about the potential diagnosis because there was not anything that I could do about it personally. I took the attitude of going with the flow, continued doing my job, and waited. What was the point of getting upset and bent out of shape over the unknown?

A few days later, I got a call from my doctor's office saying that I needed to make an appointment with a surgeon. They would not come right out and say they had found a lump, but I already knew. I went to see the surgeon, and he ordered the CT scan and had me make a follow-up appointment with him for the results. I went back in, and he told me that I did have a lump, but he did not feel it was anything to worry about. He said I could have a biopsy done now or wait six months and have it done then. I was going to wait, but my family would not let me rest in peace until I scheduled the biopsy because of the amount of cancer that runs in the family. I have to admit that it was kind of silly of me even thinking about waiting six months with my track record.

On the day I was supposed to get my results, I was unable to go because Chuck's father passed away and his funeral was that day. So we were both dealing with a double-whammy by losing his dad and the possibility of me having cancer. I called the doctor's office hoping I could get the results over the telephone, but the nurse kept telling me that I needed to come in as soon as possible but would not tell me anything. I knew 100 percent then that it was not good. I have to admit that I felt a little pitter of anxiety because I did not know exactly what I was working with. Would this tumor be a simple remove-and-treat cancer tumor, or would it be an aggressive surgery removing my breast and then fighting with chemo and radiation? Would I lose my hair, would I be able to work, or would I even survive? How far would I be willing to let the medical field go to cure me of cancer?

I finally made it to my appointment, and the doctor said yes, it was a malignant tumor and I would need surgery. By that time I had gotten over my anxiety, and all I was thinking was, *Well, let's get this show on the road and get it over with.* I did not cry, nor was I hysterical, but I felt very calm as I accepted the fact that I had cancer and it was something that had to be taken care of. I felt God had already prepared me for the horrible news of cancer. The hardest part was telling my family and coworkers that I had cancer because I knew they would be upset. They were upset on one hand, and then on the other hand, they knew that I would get through this just like everything else our family had been through. One of the concerns I had was not being able to continue to do my job and who would do it for me, as I was a one-girl office. I was quickly told not to worry about it and it would be taken care of and be there for me when I got back.

On the morning of surgery, I was told the tumor was so small that I would need a needle placement for the surgeon to know where the tumor was so he could remove it completely. How awesome that this tumor was caught in its infancy, but I couldn't help but think, with a chill up my spine, what would this tumor have been if I had waited the six months for the biopsy? Would it had been an aggressive tumor spreading into my lymph nodes? Would I have had to have my breast removed? Would I have been disfigured? What would have been my chances of survival at that time? What would my journey have been like? How would I have handled the cancer situation if I had chosen to wait? This is food for thought for anyone who might be told that they can wait for a biopsy—I say do it now.

I had my surgery, the tumor was removed, and the next day I was sent home with a drainage tube for the start of my recovery. A couple weeks later I was given an appointment to go to the oncology office to get my marking/tattoos for the radiation treatment. I find that God does have a sense of humor because I never wanted a tattoo of any shape, size, or color. My son was always saying he was going to get a tattoo someday, and I kept telling him he wasn't, yet Mom ended up being the one that was tattooed.

I had no idea what was going to take place when I went to the oncology office, and I was feeling pretty uptight, but I knew it was something I was going to have to do. Well, even though it was something I was going to have to do, it was during the marking for the radiation that I fell apart emotionally. That day, I just wanted to close my eyes and be invisible. I wanted to scream that I did not ask for this, and I wanted to blame God for making me go through this. How could anything good come out of this? I had had a lump of *cancer* removed from my body—why me? The next day the radiation was going to be blasted in my body to hopefully eliminate any stray cells that were still taking up residence in my breast area. Why? Why? Why! Was this a consequence for the path of life I had chosen? Was this God's way of saying, "I have something better for you, but I need your attention?" At that time I had such a pitiful attitude; my attention did not revolve around God.

I was scheduled for six weeks of radiation treatment, Monday through Friday. Every morning when I went in for my treatment, I hated being there, and I was very emotional. At the start of my treatments, a day did not go by that I did not cry before, during, or after the treatment. I was also so exhausted it was all I could do to function and especially when I went back to work. As weird as it may sound, I remember the first radiation treatment had zapped all the energy out of me. I returned to my office feeling like I had just been run over by a truck. I was to find out that the major fatigue, the irritability, and the tears were going to follow me through the entire treatments. I'm surprised that Chuck did not just pack his bag, or mine, until I could get control of my emotions, as I was not easy to live with!

During my daily treatments I began to recognize the people that were there for their treatments morning after morning. They would try to include me in their chitchat, but I just did not want to talk or smile to anyone. It would not sink in that they had some form of cancer just as I had; nor did it make a difference that I still had my hair because I did not have to have chemo. I eventually came around near the end of my treatments, and I starting talking and smiling to the regulars. One lady told me, "It sure is good to see you smile!" And I thought no one had really noticed or paid attention. As of the writing of this book, I am cancer free!

During the course of my radiation, we did visit a church that looked very promising, and I actually received telephone calls and e-mails from a few people at that church once they found out I was being treated for cancer. One of the ladies, whom I hardly knew, brought over dinner one evening so I would not have to cook. And yes, this is the church that I felt loved and at home in when I visited, and it is the church that I still go to today.

As I gradually eased back into a routine after my cancer treatments were completed, life was good. I was alive and now fairly healthy, going to church regularly, and enjoying life to the fullest. The years seemed to fly by, and little by little, I noticed I was not putting much of an effort in my relationship with God. I would try for a week or two, stop, and then start up again in a couple of weeks. I guess you could say I was a yo-yo Christian.

I would volunteer for things at church and then become very unreliable because "things" would get in my way. "Things" such as going out to eat, working late, being too tired, something else I felt I needed to do, working late, a haircut or doctor appointment, and working late. Oh, guess I've already said working late a couple of times, huh? However, making the choice to work late and on weekends was the main obstacle that kept me from staying in God's Word. I was also very weak spiritually, and I was doing nothing about trying to get stronger. I was still drinking milk when I should have been eating meat. I pushed the Bible aside and let it gather dust until I needed to take it to church when I finally managed to get there. I knew this way of life was not good and God was not pleased with me.

Have you ever been in a situation where you were waiting for the other shoe to drop? That is how I felt—I knew in my heart that God was going to do something to get my attention; I just did not know when, where, or how. The "something" turned out to be a very bad automobile accident that should have killed me, but it turned out to be the day when God came calling.

Chapter 4

On a beautiful sunny afternoon of April 11, 2006, at approximately five o'clock, I was slowly traveling south on the famous I-95 corridor in Stafford County, Virginia, where traffic was in a stop-and-go pattern. I was on my way to Red Lobster to wait for my husband, Chuck, to meet me there for our anniversary dinner. I knew with this traffic he would be late getting there because he leaves work after I do. I happened to glanced into my rearview mirror and saw a big truck coming up behind me a little faster than it should have been because I was stopped. I just had time for it to register in my mind, *He is going to hit me!* I remember the impact, and then with God's love and mercy, he rendered me unconscious—or so I thought.

> In my distress I called upon the Lord, and cried out to my God; he heard my voice from his temple, and my cry came before him even to his ears.
>
> Psalm 18:6

> Many times he delivered them; but they rebelled in their counsel, and were brought low for their iniquity. Nevertheless he regarded their affliction, when he heard their cry; and for their sake he remembered his covenant and relented according to the multitude of his mercies.
>
> Psalm 106:43–45

> I know, O Lord, that your judgments are right, and that in faithfulness you have afflicted me. Let, I pray, your merciful kindness be for my comfort, according to your word to your servant. Let your tender mercies come to me, that I may live, for your law is my delight.
>
> Psalm 119:75–77

I found out the next day from the state trooper that the driver of the truck had glanced down to get a soda and did not realize the traffic in front of him, which was me, had slowed down to a stop. The semi rear-ended me and ran up onto my vehicle, squished the back and sides in such a way it was barely recognizable as a car, knocked me into the pickup in front of me, and that impact knocked me over in the left lane. With traffic so heavy, I later wondered where the bumper-to-

Only by God's mercy and grace did I survive!

bumper traffic in the left lane had gone. It was as though God had cleared the left lane just for my vehicle and to avoid hitting anyone else!

The semi then rear-ended the pickup that was in front of me, knocking her into the semi in front of her. The force of the impact knocked her over in the left lane where we hit again, which knocked me over onto the embankment. When all was said and done, I was trapped in my car that looked like a crushed soda can, and everybody assumed I was dead. I was told later that there were people all around my car trying to help me, but they could not get to me because it was mangled so badly. The state trooper also said that it was really a mess when he got there, and before everything was cleared up, there was about a seven-mile backup.

The rescue squad arrived at the scene at 5:07, but it was 5:45 before they were able to get me out and start taking vitals. According to the rescue reports, they found me lying back in the driver's seat as the force of the impact had broken it into a reclining position. Guess I was as comfortable as I could be in that situation! They also indicated that my air bag did not deploy, which was another reason to praise God for his protection. It took about thirty minutes to cut me out of my mangled vehicle.

Once out, the report indicated I had difficulty breathing, and my mental status was declining. I was complaining about increased neck pain, which prompted a call for a medivac to take me to the nearest trauma center. While waiting for medivac, the rescue squad checked me over, and my lungs were clear but I started wheezing. My pupils began to slow in reaction, and I was becoming much more confused and less alert. My respirations were twenty, and at one time my BP was 133/102.

WHEN GOD CAME CALLING

Wow! This picture leaves most people speechless.

Although all reports indicated that I was somewhat alert and responding to commands, I have almost no memory of this trauma. The *only* thing I remember after the initial impact until I became aware of my surroundings in the emergency room was hearing someone say, "We're almost there," and thinking, *What is she talking about?* I did not realize that I was in a medivac and flying high in the sky on my way to the trauma center. Their report indicated that ground transport would have been hazardous due to the length of transport, which was fifty minutes versus seventeen minutes. The reason I was taken to the trauma center and not to the local hospital is because they thought I would need the trauma surgical services that were not available at the local hospital at that time. Their report indicated that I was asking repetitive questions and had no immediate recollection of the accident, which could have shown up an underlying injury to the head. According to the reports, I arrived at the trauma center at 6:17 p.m., had chest X-ray at 6:29 p.m., and had a CT scan of the head, abdomen, and cervical spine at 7:10 p.m.

I do remember bits and pieces in the emergency room between the time I arrived there and the time I was finally alert and able to talk sensibly to the doctors and nurses. I remember crying because I was in so much back pain and begging someone to give me something. They would give me pain medicine, and I would slip back into a place where there was no pain. Eventually I was finally able to answer some questions and tell them how to contact my husband. I remember that I had no idea what time it was, and I wasn't too sure what day it was; all I could remember was that I had been in a bad accident.

"The Lord is righteous in all his ways gracious in all his works. The Lord is near to all who call upon him, to all who call upon him in truth. He will fulfill the desire of those who fear him; he also will hear their cry and save them"

(Psalms 145:17–19).

As I became more aware of what was going on, I realized that I was lying on a gurney pushed up against the wall. I had been prodded and stuck, X-rayed and scanned, and was now waiting to be admitted. I had time to do a lot of thinking while lying there. One of the first things I whispered to myself was to ask God, "For what reason did this happen? What is the purpose for this accident? I know there is one." Even though my walk with God was not what it should have been and I had taken a detour from serving him, I knew this accident was part of a plan, and it was called "God's plan for Treva."

I then thanked God that I was alive, but I also told him I was very saddened that he had not gone ahead and taken me home to be with him. I had been looking forward to heaven for so long, and I really wanted to be with him. The Holy Spirit spoke to my heart, saying, "It wasn't your time," and that is when it really sunk in that since I did not die, that meant God still had a plan for me. It was with a feeling of resignation and reverent fear that I realized I had not fulfilled my purpose of why he put me on this earth. God was not finished with me, and that was very scary. I know my heart rate and blood pressure went up quite a bit, and I'm glad I was not hooked up to a monitor at that time—those nurses would have probably come running!

> Out of the depths I have cried to you, O Lord; Lord hear my voice! Let your ears be attentive to the voice of my supplications. If you, Lord, should mark iniquities; O Lord, who could stand? But *there* is forgiveness with you, that you may be feared. I wait for the Lord, my soul waits, and in his word I do hope.
>
> Psalm 130:1–5

I also felt sort of resigned to the fact that the big gloves had come out and somehow God was going to deal with me because I knew that I was not the child he wanted me to be. I had been goofing off enough, and it was time to get serious. But never would I have imagined how kind and gentle his dealings were going to be. Never would I have imagined how my heart would reabsorb his Word and his love.

I never thought that I would make the paper until my obituary, but the next day my family brought me the paper with my accident in it. It stated: "Injuries Suffered in I-95 Crash Tuesday Not Fatal."

> Neither of the two injuries suffered in a four-vehicle crash that tied up Interstate 95 during Tuesday's afternoon rush hour is life threatening, police say. The accident occurred about 5:00 p.m. Tuesday on I-95 southbound near the 136 mile-marker in Stafford County, said State Police Sgt. F. L. Tyler. A tractor-trailer hauling roofing shingles and driven by 55 year old Chase City man TLB ran into the back of a Kia driven by 52 year old Fredericksburg resident Treva Denas, Tyler said. Denas was flown to Inova Fairfax Hospital. She remained there yesterday, but police were able to interview her about the accident. Also injured in the wreck was 46 year old Stafford County resident TLM, Tyler said. Her Ford was rear-ended and she was taken to Mary Washington Hospital. The tractor-trailer also ran into a second tractor-trailer before stopping Tyler

said. Neither one of the truck drivers was injured. TLB has been charged with reckless driving. Tyler said traffic had slowed when the accident occurred. All lanes of southbound 95 were reopened by 6:30 pm. (1)

I learned later that several people from my church were in that seven-mile backup. They saw my vehicle but did not realize that it was me. After

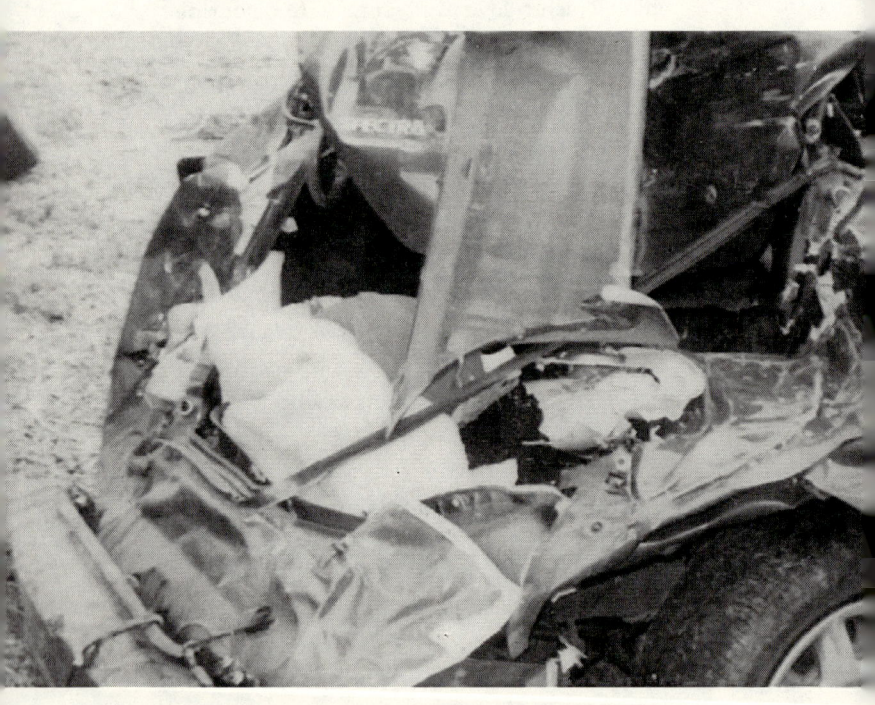

WHEN GOD CAME CALLING

Unbelievable! How was it possible that I was not critically injured?

seeing the vehicle, they all said that no one could have survived. They were very surprised to find out later it was my car and I did indeed survive! Even my husband drove by on his way to meet me at Red Lobster, but he was unable to identify the car as mine because of the damage.

Chapter 5

After spending three days in the hospital, I was able to go home with a brace to support my back. This brace would become my best friend, and I wore it at all times except when I went to bed. I had plenty of time to reflect on the accident and my life. I quickly entered into the valley of pain, tears, questions, pity parties, and depression, and I know now God held my hand through it all. But there comes a time when God has to put his foot down and help you to move on. Just like a child that is pouting because she did not get what she wanted, it was time to move on; enough was enough.

I remember a few weeks after my accident I was sitting on the couch watching TV just like I had done day after day and feeling very sorry for myself because I was barely able to do anything because of the pain. I imagine by now that God had finally gotten fed up with my pity party and decided to try and end it. I feel like he actually spoke to me because it was so powerful, but I know it was the Holy Spirit speaking to my heart trying to get a message to me. He said, "Treva, I did not save your life to have pity parties. I saved your life to praise me." The Holy Spirit spoke so clearly, and when God's words are so loud and powerful, you are either going to do an about face or run the other way and not look back, but I knew I had been running long enough. I knew that I had an attitude adjustment that needed to be made, and not only that, I also had a healthy fear of him. I knew he could still bring me down a notch or two, but he was giving me another chance. As my Bible study teacher says from time to time, "He can always take you out."

"Call upon me in the day of trouble; I will deliver you and you shall glorify me" (Psalm 10:15).

"As many as I love, I rebuke and chasten. Therefore be zealous and repent" (Revelation 3:19).

"The fear of the Lord is clean, enduring forever" (Psalm 19:9).

"Only fear the Lord, and serve him in truth with all your heart; for consider what great things he has done for you" (1 Samuel 12:24).

It was then I accepted the spiritual healing and peace similar to the peace I had when I first was saved. It was then I got reacquainted with my God. It was then I learned to fellowship with him all over again. It was then I learned to praise his holy name all over again. It was then I learned that my Heavenly Father had been waiting all this time to welcome me back into his arms all over again. It was then I learned how much my God really loved me all over again.

So I started to get reacquainted with my God, my Savior, my Lord, and my Heavenly Father. I started reading his Word every morning and having fellowship with him. I started in the book of Psalms, and it was so inspiring and uplifting. It was as if I was so thirsty and I could not get enough of the Living Water. I felt like David who had sinned and was begging for forgiveness, protection, and to be accepted again by God. I started praying about everything, not just for healing of my body and helping me through each and every day, but all the other things that would pop up such as insurance issues, car rental issues, or medical issues. Above all, I had peace of heart and peace of mind, and I felt such love from God and praised his name every day.

"I waited patiently for the Lord; and he inclined to me and heard my cry. He also brought me up out of a horrible pit, out of the miry clay; and set my feet upon a rock and established my steps" (Psalm 40:1–2).

During the time of my spiritual healing, I looked back on my life from childhood until the present, and I am totally astounded and amazed I got to where I am now. I have wondered why God hadn't just said *forget it* and turned his attention away from me. I have wondered how he is so willing to take me back again and again. I have wondered how he can still love me, believe me, or rely on me because I would make promise after promise to change and then turn right around and not keep those promises. I wondered how and why God would still want to use me—someone that was just not reliable, dependable, and did not keep her eyes on him and him alone. How many times has God picked me up, dusted me off, and stood me on the narrow road? More than I can count! You see, God has a plan with my name on it, and he has a plan with *your* name on it. He *needs us* to help carry out his plan in order that his name will be glorified! My accident is to give God the glory in all things. God gets all the credit for saving my life. I was not lucky; I was blessed! He gave me another chance because he is a God of mercy and grace.

I have found out since my accident that the driver of the pickup in front of me sustained injuries more serious then mine. I'm thinking, *How could that be?* as I was the initial impact and I received the greatest force of the hit. Again, it could only have been that God protected me from being severely injured.

> I love the Lord, because he has heard my voice and my supplications. Because he has inclined his ear to me, therefore I will call upon him as long as I live. The pains of death surrounded me, and the pangs of Sheol laid hold of me; I found trouble and sorrow. Then I called upon the name of the Lord: "O Lord I implore you, deliver my soul!" Gracious is the Lord and righteous; yes, our God is merciful. The Lord preserves the simple; I was brought low, and, he saved me.
>
> Psalms 116:1–6

> My soul, wait silently for God alone; for my expectation is from him. He only is my rock and my salvation; he is my defense, I shall

> not be moved. In God is my salvation and my glory; the rock of my strength, and my refuge, is in God. Trust in him at all times, you people; pour out your heart before him, God is a refuge for us.
>
> Psalms 62:5–8

I asked God to guide me in the kind of vehicle he wanted me to get, and that was an adventure in itself. I wasn't going to go into details about how I ended up with my Honda, but it's too good not to, so here goes.

When I was finally able to drive again, my husband and I would discuss what type of vehicle we wanted to get. Since I had a small car at the time of the accident, we wanted to check into a CR-V. We looked at all different brands because we were taking our time. It finally came down to a Honda CR-V or a Kia Sportage. I've had a Honda CR-V before and I liked it, but for some reason I really wanted the Kia. The consumer magazine gave a higher rating for the Honda, but I still wanted the Kia.

I kept praying about it and asking God to "show me." Then one morning he spoke to my heart, saying, "Treva, just as I have given you the

Bible as a road map to guide you through life, I have also allowed you to read the consumer guide. Does it not tell you which vehicle has the higher rating? Read it, child, and accept what you read."

So, even though I had the answer to my dilemma, I asked one more time, "Are you sure, Lord?"

A couple of days later, my husband came home from work and said, "We are not getting a Kia. I've seen three of them today, and they have all been on the side of the road." All right, God, I got your message loud and clear, and we got the Honda. I sometimes wonder if God has gray hair from all the grief his children give him on such simple matters. It's like "How many times do I have to tell you ... ?"

Each day is a day in which to worship God and thank him for his blessings that we all sometimes take for granted. I thank him and praise him day after day for the beautiful puffy clouds, the gorgeous sunset/sunrise, the sound of birds chirping, the beautiful blossom of a flower, the smell of fall that is in the air, and the sound of a light gentle rain. I praise him that I wake up each morning able to move and not be paralyzed. Some are such tiny blessings, but they mean so much to me because I could not have gotten a second chance. God could have taken me completely out of the picture because of my disobedience, but he chose not to.

"I will sing to the Lord as long as I live; I will sing praise to my God while I have my being. May my meditation be sweet to him, I will be glad in the Lord" (Psalms 104:33–34).

My accident taught me that whenever traffic is backed up due to an accident, I need to be more patient and not fuss but be willing to say a prayer for the people involved in the accident. You never know when it could turn out to be a family member or a close friend. To this day, whenever I hear a siren, I always say a little prayer for safety to wherever they are going.

A few weeks later, I read in our local paper an article about the sheriff's truck safety checkpoints, and it states, "Motorist fears of getting hit by trucks are valid. In a crash between an automobile and commercial truck, the damage can be devastating. You will see 75% of the people killed are in the automobile, not the truck driver, just due to sheer weight they are carrying." (2) Praise

God I was one of the 25% that survived. Percentagewise, I should be dead or severely maimed, but you know what? God does not pay attention to percentages. He had a plan, and he knew what had to be done for his plan to be carried out.

God loves us, and he does show us the path he would like us to walk, but when we make detours along the way, he will only tolerate it for a time before he does something to get our attention. Of course, we have the choice of being God's servant and doing God's will, and we have the choice of not being God's servant and not doing God's will—it is our decision. God will help us to walk the walk and talk the talk if we allow him to. However, if we flat-out refuse God's help, then he can back off and let us stumble around and see what we can do on our own. When we finally learn that we cannot handle life all by ourselves and call out to God for help, he is there to help us.

Discipline is never fun, but it usually gets us back on track with God's plan. I know that there will be times in the future that I will mess up just because I am human, and I know God will be right there prodding me to get back on the path that I got off. My goal is to keep on trying to live the life that God wants me to live and continue to praise his holy name. I really don't want another personal wake-up call from God.

"And we know that all things work together for good to those who love God, to those who are the called according to his purpose" (Romans 8:28).

God blessed me in many ways in this horrific accident. Looking back, I see many ways God showed me his mercy and love during the actual accident and my recovery, and I have listed some of them below:

1. He allowed me to not remember anything after the initial impact. I was trapped in the vehicle and could not move because of all the jagged glass and twisted metal. I cannot stand being unable to move, and I would have gone into hysterics if I had been conscious.

2. If I had been able to move, I could have caused my injury of a broken vertebra to end up being more serious than it was.

3. Once they found out I was alive, they ordered a medivac helicopter, stat, to take me to the hospital. I *do not* fly. I was and still am petrified of flying. Again, in God's

wisdom, he knew if I was aware of what was going on that I would have freaked out knowing I was being put on a helicopter.

4. I don't remember when the medical personnel attempted to start IVs and to get blood work. I wasn't coherent enough to tell them that my left arm was normally off limits due to a lumpectomy I had for the breast cancer. I was not able to tell them that my veins were very small and hard to find, but by the looks of my arms in the days that followed, I'm assuming they found that out. My arms were black and blue for days because of them trying to find a vein. If I had been aware of my surroundings, I would have probably slapped someone for sticking me several times to find a vein.

5. I do not remember when the medical personnel were cutting off my clothes after I got to the hospital, and it does happen just like they show on TV! I was not very happy about that because I had just recently bought that outfit, and it was the first time I wore it.

6. I see God's blessings through my children who rushed to my bedside as soon as they received the phone call. My daughter immediately took a week off to be with me and to help take care of me.

7. I see God's blessings through my sister when I was able to call her the next morning after my accident. I left a message on her cell phone at work, and within an hour of getting that message, all family members knew about my accident and were in constant prayer for my recovery.

8. I see God's blessing that the pastor made a trip all the way up north just to see me after he had been alerted of the accident.

9. I see God's blessing in my church family who immediately starting praying for me when they found out about the accident. I also see God's blessing in my church family who called me, visited me, sent me cards, brought me food, and showed their Christian love and support to me.

10. I see God's blessing when someone just happens to ask, "Are you doing okay financially? If not, I expect you to let me know."

11. I see God's blessing when others look at the pictures of the vehicle and they start praising God because they realize that God was truly with me at the time of the accident. As someone told me, "God held you in his arms and protected you from death." Just picture that in your mind of God holding you to protect you from harm!

12. I see God's blessing when people look at the pictures and they are encouraged because they're "seeing" God at work. They are seeing something that God had a hand in, and they have a confirmation that God is very real and does love us.

    "From the rising of the sun to its going down the Lord's name is to be praised" (Psalm 113:3).

13. I see God's blessing when I looked over my shirt I had hanging in the car at the time of the accident, and even with all the twisted metal and broken glass, there was not a rip or a smudge of dirt on the shirt.

14. I see God's blessing when I know that I should have been critically injured because of the severity of the accident. *God is so merciful and good!*
15. I see God's blessing, and humor, when I was finally able to bend down enough to shave my legs! If I had to wait much longer, I would have had to get a Bush Hog to use! Sorry, guys, if this is too much information!

Chapter 6

Since the accident, I have asked different people that were either EMTs or rescue responders if they had been the ones to handle my accident, what would they have thought my injuries could have been due to the severity of the crash? Some said it would be a given that the occupant would have multiple injuries. Mental status decrease could have indicated some type of head injury. Difficulty in breathing and wheezing could have indicated a fractured rib and/or a collapsed lung. Another person said that he would have suspected brain, head, and/or spinal cord injuries. However, God was merciful to me, and the only injuries I ended up with were a T11 vertebrae fracture, bruised ribs, a concussion, and a couple of abrasions.

I ask you to take a good look at the pictures of my car and then try to tell yourself that God was not there with me. He not only saved my life, but he protected me from several serious life-threatening injuries. *Praise God!*

God loved me so much that he just could not let me continue on the path I was on. He knew I had a tender heart toward him; I just needed a tune-up. It does not matter what we are going through; God loves us. It does not matter how large our burdens are; God is bigger! He only wants us to praise him for the blessings he gives to us every day. He wants us to trust him as he leads us through the valleys and over the mountaintops, but we can only trust him if our hearts are filled with his love for us and our love for him.

I know that some of you are going through rough times right now or your heart has grown lukewarm or cold because of your neglect of God. You think you don't have what it takes to serve God. Or "what's the use?" Or "I can never get it right because I'm okay for a few weeks and then I fall again." Well, that's okay, because God will be right there picking you back up if you let him. Plus, you have to remember that it's not God telling you these things; it's Satan. God would never make you feel worthless and useless; only Satan would stoop as low as that. You will *never* lose your value in God's eyes; he loves you too much! Psalm 17:8 states that God will keep us "as the apple of his eye."

Do you feel you are worthless and will never amount to anything? Do you lack the peace that passeth all understanding? People know in their hearts what is right and what is wrong. God is ready to show mercy and grace to anyone who wants to turn from what is wrong to what is right.

Are you worried about someone or something? The only purpose for worry is to indicate to us that we need to turn our problems over to God. Once we enlist the help of our Lord, then we can rest—God will carry us through any situation, and he will grant us peace of mind and peace of heart! Have you pushed God into a closet and shut the door instead of allowing him to reside in your heart and soul?

They say that hindsight is 20/20, and sometimes I think a lot of *what-ifs*. I've done a lot of things that I am very ashamed of, that I wished I had never done, and that I would like the opportunity to do over. But if I could—I wonder if the choices I would make would be any better, or would they be worse than what I actually did? I just wished I had not dilly-dallied around with God but really trusted him instead of taking matters into my own hands.

I so much regret not leaning on my God, not talking to my God, not listening to my God, and not allowing my God to provide and show me the future he wanted me to have. I so regret the blessings my children and I have missed because of my disobedience. Even though there are times that I still feel so worthless because of my past, I know God does not see me that way. The past is forgiven, over with, and done with. The future is where everything that's going to happen to you from this moment on is going to take place.

"For I will be merciful to their unrighteousness and their sins and their lawless deeds I will remember no more" (Hebrews 8:12).

"I, even I, am he who blots out your transgressions for my own sake; And I will not remember your sins" (Isaiah 43:25).

If we truly ask God for his forgiveness and God does not remember our past, why should we? We normally learn from our mistakes, and if we have to do a small walk down memory lane now and then and feel the sorrows, the disappointments, the hurts, the pains, and the what-ifs, that's okay, but don't plan on staying there for any length of time. You need to remember that Satan will crash your memory-lane party, and it will turn into a long, extended vacation instead of the short, pop-in visit you had in mind. God is about now!

I know that God can take situations that we find ourselves in and turn them around when we finally come to our senses and ask God for his forgiveness, mercy, and grace. Sometimes he will find a way to use it in our lives as a way to help others and to glorify him. As the saying goes, "Only God can undo what I have begun" and open a different road of opportunity.

> Therefore, having been justified by faith, we have peace with God through our Lord Jesus Christ, through whom also we have access by faith into this grace in which we stand and rejoice in the hope of the glory of God. And not only that, but we also glory in tribulations, knowing that tribulation produces perseverance; and perseverance, character; and character, hope. Now hope does not disappoint, because the love of God has been poured out in our hearts by the Holy Spirit who was given us.
> Romans 5:1–5

Perhaps your soul is not a pretty picture either. Perhaps you are still beating yourself up over the past. Perhaps you are feeling worthless, unloved, full of self-pity, and depressed. Don't be; God is there for you so don't give up, but take his hand and fight. You cannot lose! You can only win! You may be saying, "But if God only knew what I've done..." Well, he does, and he still wants you to come back to him, ask for his forgiveness, and to be forgiven. He's waiting with open arms. I know because he has taken me back into his arms so many times, and he never loved me any less. The key is to talk and walk with God every day. Read his holy Word and apply his directions to your life. Tell him about every problem, no matter how minor or silly, and let him help you. Christian life is like learning to ride a bicycle—if you fall off, get up and keep trying.

Remember the story in Luke 15:4–7:

> What man of you having a hundred sheep, if he loses one of them, does not leave the ninety nine in the wilderness and go after the one which is lost until he finds it? And when he has found it, he lays it on his shoulders, rejoicing. And when he comes homes, he calls

together his friends and neighbors, saying to them, "Rejoice with me, for I have found my sheep which was lost! I say to you that likewise there will be more joy in heaven over one sinner who repents than over ninety nine just persons who need no repentance."

God is like that, and we are all his *one little lamb* from time to time. Perhaps you realize you have never invited Jesus into your heart or you are not sure; well, now is the time. Ask Jesus into your heart; ask him to forgive you of your sins and make you a new creature in Christ. Believe that he died for our sins, arose from the dead on the third day, and will come back to get his children one day, maybe today. Personally, I cannot wait for that day! So grab hold of God's never-ending love and mercy for you and be willing to start a new journey down your road of life with God being the driver. Don't keep avoiding and ignoring God like I did and let a semi come flying up behind you. You have got to keep in mind that perhaps God has a wake-up call with your name on it if needed. Don't put off becoming a child of God; do it now and meet me in heaven one day. God bless!

"Praise the Lord! Praise the Lord, O my soul! While I live I will praise the Lord; I will sing praises to my God while I have my being" (Psalm 146:1–2).

Epilogue

03/2009—It has been almost three years since the day when God came calling. I would love to say that my walk with God has been without falter, but it has not. It was with dread that I returned to work after my accident because I just knew that my cherished relationship I had with God during my recovery would be severely tested. I was right, and before I knew it, I was back working twelve to fourteen hours a day and some weekends. It was very stressful and disheartening to watch and feel my one-on-one relationship with God slowly slipping away. Don't get me wrong; I was not anywhere near where I was when God originally came calling, but I was creeping farther and farther from his plan and blessings. This time around, I did not want to be farther and farther from his plan and blessings. This time around, I *yearned* to talk to God one on one and to be obedient to his plans. How could I praise him if I was working all the time and totally exhausted?

It got to the point that my heart just ached because I was missing my close relationship with God so much. I knew I had the assurance of my salvation and that God was still with me, but work was crowding him out. Most mornings I would arrive at work early and take a few minutes to stand in front of my window and watch the beautiful sunrises that God sent and praise him for his creation. I would also shed tears of desperation and sadness because I felt trapped and not able to give my all to God, but I just did not see a way out or know what to do. On some mornings, I would just cry and tell God that I could not handle another stressful day, and I would end up having a busy but serene day. That really encouraged me, when God heard me calling to him to help me get through the day. I knew that God was the same yesterday, today, and tomorrow. I knew he would be waiting for my one on one with him each morning as I watched the beautiful sunrises he created.

One summer morning, I was standing at my office window drinking my coffee and watching one of God's stunning sunrises. I was feeling so very, very tired, both physically and emotionally, and on that day, God and I had a little chitchat that changed everything. I will share it below.

Me: "God, I cannot serve you and work too."

God: "And?"

Me: "And?"

God: "What are you going to do about it?"

Me: "Well...I could quit work."

God: "Okay."

Me: "Okay? Um...when do you propose that I quit?"

God: "The end of the year."

Me: "I...um...Okay, Father."

"Trust in the Lord with all your heart, and lean not on your own understanding; in all your ways acknowledge him and he shall direct your paths" (Proverbs 3:5–6).

That was the essence of our conversation, and after the initial realization of what I just did kicked in, I had such sweet peace with it. That is the only reason that I retired when I did because

God came calling and saved my life to praise him. But with me working like I was, I was putting my job before God and allowing it to interfere with the reason that God saved my life.

Some people have the capability and discipline to do their jobs and go home when it is quitting time regardless of what is left lying on their desks. I did not have that attitude or discipline, and I felt I needed to make a dent in the stacks on my desk. The only way I could do that was to work late when everyone had gone home and there were no more interruptions.

Am I telling you that you need to quit your job to serve God? Nope! Not unless God tells you to. Just don't put your job before God; God is a jealous God.

"For the Lord your God is a consuming fire, a jealous God" (Deuteronomy 4:24).

God and my relationship with him was now my number one priority. I knew financially things would be tight as we made the adjustment from two incomes to one. However, I also knew God would provide and we would have what we needed, and he has.

And how did my husband take the news that I was going to retire? After much discussion, he said for me to do what I felt the Lord wanted me to do and we would make it somehow. He also realizes this book is God's book, not Treva's, and both of us are waiting to see where it will lead. He has come to see, know, and accept that God saved my life in the accident and realizes God has something for me to do. Chuck continues to go to church with me most Sundays but has not yet made his statement of faith. I realize his commitment is between him and God, and I no longer nag him about it. I can only try to live a life that is pleasing to the Lord and continue to pray for Chuck to make that commitment before it's too late as he continues to learn more and more about this *God thing!*

Today, Chuckie is an adult, and as he matured and grew up, he got his driver's license, graduated from high school, got a good job, and got married. They had a daughter—my first granddaughter—bought a house with a big yard, and moved out in the country. I'm sorry to say that their marriage did not survive and they eventually divorced. He works hard for what he has, seems to have a good head on his shoulders, and he's always there to help out when needed. Even though he is my stepson, I consider him a son. I continue to pray that he finds a Bible-teaching, preaching church and to be obedient to God's calling.

Today, Dwayne is an adult, and as he matured and grew up, he quit school, had issues, got his driver's license, got a job with a grocery store chain, and got married. The grocery store chain reorganized and moved their stores out of the Roanoke area to North Carolina. My son and his wife decided to move to North Carolina so they could stay with the store. Their son, my first grandson, was born there, and when their year was up, they moved back to the Roanoke area. I'm sorry to say that their marriage did not survive, and they eventually went their separate ways. My son works with a plumbing company and enjoys working with his hands. He also has his issues, and a lot of his issues are caused by a quick tongue and stubbornness. I continue to pray that he returns to a Bible-teaching, preaching church in his area and to be obedient to God's calling.

Today, I praise God that my son does not remember the horrible tantrums and behavior problems that I had with him. I praise God even more that he does not remember the time he almost hit me with a baseball bat in a fit of anger but missed me and broke the window instead. It was so heartbreaking to see my sunshine baby turn into such a hateful, tantrum-throwing, aggressive, and angry young boy. I praise God that he has matured into an adult with a good job and a roof over his head. Of course, he's not perfect, and he still does things that I don't agree with. I've asked him if he remembers anything about this childhood, and he said, "I don't remember a lot about my childhood except things were really bad."

Today, Melissa is an adult, and as she matured and grew up, she was able to get her driver's license, graduate from high school, and get a job working with children while going to a community college. She graduated from college and is now working as a family case manager with an organization in Roanoke, Virginia. She has her own personality and qualities that I find so awesome. I continue to pray that she will return to a Bible-teaching, preaching church in her area and to be obedient to God's calling.

Today, I praise God for my daughter who has matured into a loving, nurturing, kind, and determined young lady. A lot of people say that she's just like me, and I haven't decided if that is good or bad! I praise God that she has a level head on her shoulders even though she has been through a lot. She is a very strong person, and she uses her mothering instinct to mother her mother, and I enjoy almost every minute of it. I praise God that she was determined not to let her childhood miseries get the best of her, and she graduated from high school and college. She has had a lot of physical issues and suffers from severe back pain, and it is very hard for me to see and hear that she is suffering. I know I cannot do anything but pray that God will give her strength to handle the pain or to take it completely away.

As she is older, she remembers a lot of things that went on, and we recently had a little talk about it. Below is our conversation.

> I asked her, "How did you feel when your dad left us?"
> She said, "That was so long ago that I do not remember much about it. I do remember that I was upset that I was told by someone other than you, someone at church. [Note: I did not know this.] I thought that things would be better with Dad gone, that maybe we would

see him more, but that did not happen. I remember not having money for the simple things and having to have the church provide us food, clothing, etc."

I asked her, "Did you feel like I had abandoned you?"
She said, "Yes, I did not want to stay with Dad as Dwayne was already there most of the time. So the only option was to go live with Granny. This was difficult as I was not used to living that far out in the country. Not only was I losing my mom, but I had to leave my friends, many I had since kindergarten. This was a big adjustment."

I asked her, "Did you hate me when I left?"
She said, "No."

I asked her, "Do you feel that you accomplished more by living with Granny, such as graduating from high school and college?"
She said, "I would like to think I would have gone to college anywhere I was but do not know that for sure. I think it would have been easier if you had been here as I had to move in with Dad again so I could go to school and not have to drive back and forth."

> I asked her, "Why did you not want to go with me? Was it because of the distance and you would be far away from your dad and Granny?" She said, "I am not sure why I did not go with you; I just remember that not being an option."
>
> I asked her, "Do you think that you are a stronger person because of what you/we went through with your dad leaving, then Dwayne turning into a brat, and my relationships?"
> She said, "I do think I am a stronger person. I feel that I am better at my job, and I can relate to many of my moms that are doing the same thing or have gone through the same things that I have. I can also give them the point of view as a child who went through divorce and the parents' other relationships."

It is such a blessing to see that God could use all of the turmoil, hurts, tears, heartaches, and sadness and turn it into something that allows my son, my daughter, and me to use to help others to this day. When we say, "I know how you feel" or "I know what you are going through," we really do know.

Oh, remember earlier in the book how I felt when the church intervened and confronted me about my living situation? In case you don't, it was

"How dare they!" But I will have to say that once I got my act together years later I realized they were right! Praise God that they were obedient to God's Word and came to me to talk about my situation and that I needed to rethink what I was doing. I was living in a sinful situation that did not honor God, not to mention the example I was setting for my children, the youth group, and the young unmarried people within my church. The church *had* to take action because I was a threat to the unity of the church and God's teaching on purity. The Bible plainly tells us what has to be done in these types of circumstances. I am so thankful that my church had the backbone and love to do what they did.

> Moreover if your brother sins against you, go and tell him his fault between you and him alone. If he hears you, you have gained your brother. But if he will not hear, take with you one or two more, that "by the mouth of two or three witnesses every word may be established." And if he refuses to hear them, tell it to the church. But if he refuses even to hear the church, let him be to you like a heathen and a tax collector.
>
> Matthew 18:15–17

> Do not be deceived, God is not mocked; for whatever a man sows, that he will also reap. For he who sows to his flesh will of the flesh reap corruption, but he who sows to the Spirit will of the Spirit reap everlasting life.
>
> Galatians 6:7–8

My heart still gets very, very sad when I think about the loss of the special bond that KL and I had. She was my best friend, my confidant, my coffee partner, my phone partner, and my shoulder to cry on. We were *always* there for each other and would drop everything just to help one another out. I will never be able to forget her because she was the one that invited me to church and was with me when I accepted Jesus Christ. However, because of my choices and the life *I chose* to live, I lost KL's true friendship. Thinking about it now, I know she was also saddened because I was living in a situation that was totally wrong. At the time it really did not matter, but now that I have my life back in God's hands, it does matter. It has been almost twenty years since I gave up my friendship with KL, and I still think about her often and what a special bond God had blessed us with, but I threw it away—by choice.

God did not save my soul about thirty-three years ago to get off on the wrong track and stay there. He created me not to sit on the sidelines but to be willing to participate in his plan, for God does have a plan for each of us. He saved my soul to serve him, not to feel worthless. We need to remember that the worth of our lives comes not in what we do or who we are, but by *whose we are!* It took a traumatic auto accident to get me to *finally* quit being so stubborn and to wake up and listen to what God wants me to do. It indeed was the day when God came calling.

As stated earlier in this book, God saved my life not to have pity parties but to praise him, and I feel this book has accomplished that.

> Take control of my words today,
> May they tell of your great love;
> And may the story of your grace
> Turn some heart to you above.

TREVA DENAS

"I can do all things through Christ who strengthens me" (Philippians 4:13).

Bibliography

1. Bill Freehling, Free Lance Star Newspaper, April 13, 2006

2. Kelly Hannon, Free Lance Star Newspaper, January 27, 2007

e|LIVE

listen|imagine|view|experience

AUDIO BOOK DOWNLOAD INCLUDED WITH THIS BOOK!

In your hands you hold a complete digital entertainment package. Besides purchasing the paper version of this book, this book includes a free download of the audio version of this book. Simply use the code listed below when visiting our website. Once downloaded to your computer, you can listen to the book through your computer's speakers, burn it to an audio CD or save the file to your portable music device (such as Apple's popular iPod) and listen on the go!

How to get your free audio book digital download:

1. Visit www.tatepublishing.com and click on the e|LIVE logo on the home page.
2. Enter the following coupon code:
   b956-8a7c-2b74-3229-d3cb-09d2-01b2-451c
3. Download the audio book from your e|LIVE digital locker and begin enjoying your new digital entertainment package today!